Fast Breakfast

Instant Pot Breakfast Recipes for Families

David Walton

Sommario

Introduction

This full and also helpful overview to instantaneous pot food preparation with over 1000 recipes for morning meal, supper, dinner, and also treats! This is one of one of the most comprehensive split second pot cookbooks ever before released thanks to its variety and accurate guidelines. Innovative dishes and classics, modern take on family members's most loved meals-- all this is yummy, easy as well as certainly as healthy as it can be. Change the means you cook with these cutting-edge immediate pot guidelines. Need a new supper or a dessert? Here you are! Ideal immediate pot dishes come together in a few easy steps, even a novice can do it! The instantaneous pot defines the way you prepare daily. This immediate pot recipe book aids you make the absolute most out of your regular food selection. The only immediate pot book you will certainly ever before need with the ultimate collection of recipes will certainly assist you in the direction of a simpler and much healthier kitchen area experience. If you wish to conserve time cooking meals a lot more effectively, if you intend to use your family members food that can please also the pickiest eater, you are in the best area! Master your immediate pot and also make your cooking requires match your hectic way of living.

Breakfast recipes

Fragrant Coffee

Prep time: 10 minutes

Cooking time: 5 minutes

Servings: 4

Ingredients:

- 4 teaspoon butter

- 2 cups of water

- 4 teaspoons instant coffee

- 1 tablespoon Erythritol

- 1/3 cup heavy cream

- 1 teaspoon ground cinnamon

- ½ teaspoon vanilla extract

Directions:

1. Pour water, heavy cream, ground cinnamon, and vanilla extract in the cooker.

2. Add instant coffee and stir well until homogenous.

3. Close and seal the lid.

4. Cook the coffee mixture on high-pressure mode for 4 minutes.

5. Then allow natural pressure release for 10 minutes.

6. Open the lid and add butter. Stir well and pour coffee in the serving cups.

Nutrition: calories 71, fat 7.5, fiber 0.3, carbs 0.8, protein 0.3

Veggie Egg Cups

Prep time: 5 minutes

Cooking time: 7 minutes

Servings: 4

Ingredients:

- 1 zucchini

- 2 tablespoon almond flour

- ½ teaspoon salt

- 1 teaspoon butter

- 4 eggs

Directions:

1. Grate zucchini and mix it up with almond flour and salt.

2. Spread the muffin molds with butter and place grated zucchini inside in the shape of nests.

3. Then beat eggs inside "zucchini nests" and place them in the cooker.

4. Lower the air fryer lid.

5. Cook the zucchini cups for 7 minutes.

6. When the eggs are solid, the meal is cooked.

Nutrition: calories 99, fat 7.2, fiber 0.9, carbs 2.7, protein 6.9

Egg Fluffs

Prep time: 10 minutes

Cooking time: 6 minutes

Servings: 4

Ingredients:

- 4 egg whites

- ½ teaspoon lemon juice

- ½ teaspoon salt

- 1 teaspoon almond flour

Directions:

1. Whisk the egg whites with lemon juice until strong peaks.

2. Add salt and almond flour. Stir it.

3. Place the egg white clouds in the cooker with the help of the spoon.

4. Lower the air fryer lid.

5. Cook the egg clouds for 6 minutes or until they are light brown.

Nutrition: calories 21, fat 0.4, fiber 0.1, carbs 0.4, protein 3.7

Avocado Bacon Bombs

Prep time: 10 minutes

Cooking time: 10 minutes

Servings: 4

Ingredients:

- 1 avocado, peeled, cored
- 4 oz bacon, sliced
- 1 tablespoon almond flour
- 1 tablespoon flax meal
- ½ teaspoon salt

Directions:

1. Blend together avocado, almond flour, flax meal, and salt.

2. When the mixture is smooth, transfer it in the mixing bowl.

3. Make the medium size balls from it and wrap in the bacon.

4. Secure the balls with the toothpicks.

5. After this, transfer the bombs in the cooker and ser air crisp mode.

6. Close the lid and cook the meal for 10 minutes.

Nutrition: calories 303, fat 25.8, fiber 4.6, carbs 6.7, protein 13.3

Pepper Avocado

Prep time: 15 minutes

Cooking time: 10 minutes

Servings: 2

Ingredients:

- 1 avocado, halved
- 2 eggs
- ½ teaspoon ground black pepper
- 1 teaspoon butter

Directions:

1. Beat the eggs in the avocado halves, sprinkle with ground black pepper.

2. Then add butter.

3. Add 1 cup of water in the cooker.

4. Transfer the avocado halves on the trivet in the Foodi Pressure cooker and close the lid.

5. Cook the breakfast for 10 minutes on High-pressure mode.

6. Then allow natural pressure release for 10 minutes.

Nutrition: calories 286, fat 25.2, fiber 6.9, carbs 9.3, protein 7.5

Creamy Omelet

Prep time: 10 minutes

Cooking time: 7 minutes

Servings: 4

Ingredients:

- 4 eggs, whisked
- ¼ cup cream
- ½ teaspoon salt
- 2 oz bacon, chopped
- 1 teaspoon butter, melted
- 1 cup water, for cooking

Directions:

1. Mix up together whisked eggs, cream, salt, and chopped bacon.

2. Add melted butter and stir the mixture.

3. Pour egg mixture in the mason jars.

4. Pour 1 cup of water in the Pressure cooker and insert trivet.

5. Place mason jars on the trivet.

6. Close the lid and cook an omelet for 7 minutes on High-pressure mode.

7. Then use quick pressure release. Chill the meal little before serving.

Nutrition: calories 234, fat 18, fiber 0, carbs 1.2, protein 16.2

Flax Pancake

Prep time: 10 minutes

Cooking time: 10 minutes

Servings: 2

Ingredients:

- 7 oz cauliflower
- 2 eggs, whisked
- 2 tablespoons almond flour
- 1 tablespoon flax meal
- 1 teaspoon butter
- 1 teaspoon chili flakes
- 1 teaspoon dried dill

Directions:

1. Grind the cauliflower and mix it up with the whisked eggs, almond flour, flax meal, chili flakes, and dried dill.

2. Stir the mixture well.

3. Preheat Foodi cooker on saute mode and add butter. Melt it.

4. Place cauliflower mixture in the cooker with the help of the spoon (to get pancake shape) and cook for 4 minutes from each side.

Nutrition: calories 161, fat 11.2, fiber 4.3, carbs 8.4, protein 9.9

Almond Eggs

Prep time: 5 minutes

Cooking time: 9 minutes

Servings: 5

Ingredients:

- 7 eggs

- ½ cup almond milk

- 1 tablespoon butter

- 1 teaspoon basil

- ¼ cup fresh parsley

- 1 teaspoon salt

- 1 teaspoon paprika

- 4 ounces sliced bacon

- 1 tablespoon cilantro

Directions:

1. Beat the eggs in a mixing bowl and whisk well.

2. Add the almond milk, basil, salt, paprika, and cilantro. Stir the mixture well.

3. Chop the bacon and parsley.

4. Set the pressure cooker mode to "Sauté" and add the bacon. Cook it for 3 minutes.

5. Add the whisked egg mixture, and cook for 5 additional minutes.

6. Stir the eggs carefully using a wooden spoon or spatula.

7. Sprinkle the eggs with the chopped parsley, and cook it for 4 minutes.

8. When the eggs are cooked, remove them from the pressure cooker.

Nutrition: calories 289, fat 23.7, fiber 0.8, carbs 2.6, protein 16.9

Avocado Eggs

Prep time: 15 minutes

Cooking time: 15 minutes

Servings: 6

Ingredients:

- 2 cups of water

- 1 avocado, pitted

- 4 eggs

- 1 teaspoon paprika

- ½ teaspoon ground black pepper

- 1 sweet bell pepper

- 1 teaspoon salt

- 3 tablespoons heavy cream

- 3 ounces lettuce leaves

Directions:

1. Put the eggs and water in the pressure cooker and close the lid.

2. Set the pressure cooker mode to "Pressure," and cook for 15 minutes.

3. Remove the eggs from the pressure cooker, and transfer them to an ice bath.

4. Chop the avocado, and remove the seeds from bell pepper.

5. Dice the bell peppers and Peel the eggs and chop them.

6. Combine the chopped ingredients together in a mixing bowl.

7. Sprinkle the mixture with the paprika, ground black pepper, salt, and stir.

8. Transfer the mixture in the lettuce leaves, sprinkle them with the cream, and serve.

Nutrition: calories 168, fat 12.9, fiber 3, carbs 6.75, protein 7

Cheddar Migas

Prep time: 10 minutes

Cooking time: 10 minutes

Servings: 6

Ingredients:

- 10 eggs

- 1 jalapeno pepper

- 8 ounces tomatoes

- 1 tablespoon chicken stock

- 7 ounces cheddar cheese

- 2 white onions

- 2 cups tortilla chips

- 1 sweet bell pepper

- ½ cup beef stock

- 1 teaspoon salt

Directions:

1. Whisk the eggs in the mixing bowl.

2. Chop the jalapeno peppers and tomatoes.

3. Grate the cheddar cheese.

4. Peel the onions and chop them.

5. Crush the tortilla chips. Chop the bell peppers.

6. Combine the jalapeno pepper, tomatoes, onion, and chopped bell pepper together and stir the mixture.

7. Set the pressure cooker mode to "Sauté", and transfer the vegetable mixture.

8. Cook it for 5 minutes.

9. Add the whisked eggs mixture.

10. Add the stocks, salt, and grated cheese. Mix up the mixture well, and cook it for 4 minutes.

11. Add the crushed tortilla chips, and cook for 1 minute more.

12. Stir it and serve.

13.   Note: Only add salt if using low-sodium chicken and beef stock; otherwise, you can omit the salt.!

Nutrition: calories 295, fat 19.3, fiber 1, carbs 9.27, protein 21

Soft Eggs

Prep time: 7 minutes

Cooking time: 7 minutes

Servings: 4

Ingredients:

- 7 ounces sliced bacon

- 4 eggs, boiled

- 1 teaspoon cilantro

- ½ cup spinach

- 2 teaspoons butter

- ½ teaspoon ground white pepper

- 3 tablespoons heavy cream

Directions:

1. Lay the bacon flat and sprinkle it with the ground white pepper and cilantro on both sides of the slices and stir the mixture.

2. Peel the eggs, and wrap them in the spinach leaves.

3. Wrap the eggs in the sliced bacon.

4. Set the pressure cooker mode to "Sauté" and transfer the wrapped eggs.

5. Add butter and cook for 10 minutes.

6. When the cooking time ends, remove the eggs from the pressure cooker and sprinkle them with the cream.

7. Serve the dish immediately.

Nutrition: calories 325, fat 28.4, fiber 2, carbs 5.24, protein 15

Creamy Soufflé

Prep time: 10 minutes

Cooking time: 20 minutes

Servings: 6

Ingredients:

- 3 eggs

- 1 cup cream

- 6 ounces of cottage cheese

- 4 tablespoons butter

- ⅓ cup dried apricots

- 1 tablespoon sour cream

- 2 tablespoons sugar

- 1 teaspoon vanilla extract

Directions:

1. Whisk the eggs and combine them with cream.

2. Transfer the cottage cheese to a mixing bowl, and mix it well using a hand mixer.

3. Add the whisked eggs, butter, sour cream, sugar, and vanilla extract.

4. Blend the mixture well until smooth.

5. Add the apricots, and stir the mixture well.

6. Transfer the soufflé in the pressure cooker and close the lid. Set the pressure cooker mode to «Sauté», and cook for 20 minutes.

7. When the cooking time ends, let the soufflé cool little and serve.

Nutrition: calories 266, fat 21.1, fiber 1, carbs 11.72, protein 8

Zucchini Casserole

Prep time: 10 minutes

Cooking time: 30 minutes

Servings: 8

Ingredients:

- 6 ounces cheddar cheese
- 1 zucchini
- ½ cup ground chicken
- 4 ounces Parmesan cheese
- 3 tablespoons butter
- 1 teaspoon paprika
- 1 teaspoon salt
- 1 teaspoon basil
- 1 teaspoon cilantro
- ½ cup fresh dill
- ⅓ cup tomato juice

- ½ cup cream

- 2 red sweet bell peppers

Directions:

1. Grate cheddar cheese.

2. Chop the zucchini and combine it with the ground chicken.

3. Sprinkle the mixture with the paprika, salt, basil, cilantro, tomato juice, and cream. Stir the mixture well. Transfer it to the pressure cooker.

4. Chop the dill, sprinkle the mixture in the pressure cooker, and add the butter. Chop the Parmesan cheese and add it to the pressure cooker.

5. Chop the bell peppers and add them too. Sprinkle the mixture with the grated cheddar cheese and close the lid.

6. Set the pressure cooker mode to "Sauté", and cook for 30 minutes.

7. When the cooking time ends, let the casserole chill briefly and serve.

Nutrition: calories 199, fat 14.7, fiber 1, carbs 6.55, protein 11

Spinach Casserole

Prep time: 6 minutes

Cooking time: 6 minutes

Servings: 5

Ingredients:

- 2 cups spinach

- 8 eggs

- ½ cup almond milk

- 1 teaspoon salt

- 1 tablespoon olive oil

- 1 teaspoon ground black pepper

- 4 ounces Parmesan cheese

Directions:

1. Add the eggs to a mixing bowl and whisk them.

2. Chop the spinach and add it to the egg mixture.

3. Add the almond milk, salt, olive oil, and ground black pepper. Stir the mixture well. Transfer the egg mixture to the pressure cooker and close the lid.

4. Set the pressure cooker mode to "Steam," and cook for 6 minutes.

5. Grate the cheese. When the cooking time ends, remove the omelet from the pressure cooker and transfer it to a serving plate.

6. Sprinkle the dish with the grated cheese and serve.

Nutrition: calories 257, fat 20.4, fiber 0.9, carbs 3.4, protein 17.1

Spicy Romano Bites

Prep time: 6 minutes

Cooking time: 20 minutes

Servings: 8

Ingredients:

- 10 ounces Romano cheese

- 6 ounces sliced bacon

- 1 teaspoon oregano

- 5 ounces puff pastry

- 1 teaspoon butter

- 2 egg yolks

- 1 teaspoon sesame seeds

Directions:

1. Chop Romano cheese into small cubes.

2. Roll the puff pastry using a rolling pin. Whisk the egg yolks.

3. Sprinkle them with the oregano and sesame seeds.

4. Cut the puff pastry into the squares, and place an equal amount of butter on every square. Wrap the cheese cubes in the sliced bacon.

5. Place the wrapped cheese cubes onto the puff pastry squares. Make the "bites" of the dough and brush them with the egg yolk mixture.

6. Transfer the bites in the pressure cooker.

7. Close the lid, and set the pressure cooker mode to "Steam." Cook for 20 minutes.

8. When the cooking time ends, remove the dish from the pressure cooker and place on a serving dish.

Nutrition: calories 321, fat 24.4, fiber 1, carbs 10.9, protein 16

Eggs and Chives

Prep time: 4 minutes

Cooking time: 4 minutes

Servings: 3

Ingredients:

- 3 eggs

- 6 ounces ham

- 1 teaspoon salt

- ½ teaspoon ground white pepper

- 1 teaspoon paprika

- ¼ teaspoon ground ginger

- 2 tablespoons chives

Directions:

1. Take three small ramekins and coat them with vegetable oil spray.

2. Beat the eggs add an equal amount to the ramekins. Sprinkle the eggs with the salt, ground black pepper, and paprika.

3. Transfer the ramekins to the pressure cooker and set the mode to "Steam."

4. Close the lid, and cook for 4 minutes. Meanwhile, chop the ham and chives and combine them.

5. Add ground ginger and stir into the ham mixture well. Transfer the mixture to the serving plates.

6. When the cooking time ends, remove the eggs from the pressure cooker and put them atop the ham mixture.

Nutrition: calories 205, fat 11.1, fiber 1, carbs 6.47, protein 19

Zucchini Quiche

Prep time: 15 minutes

Cooking time: 40 minutes

Servings: 6

Ingredients:

- 3 green zucchini
- 7 ounces puff pastry
- 2 onions
- 1 cup dill
- 2 eggs
- 3 tablespoons butter
- ½ cup cream
- 6 ounces cheddar cheese
- 1 teaspoon salt
- 1 teaspoon paprika

Directions:

1. Wash the zucchini and grate the vegetables.

2. Peel the onions and chop them. Grate the cheddar cheese.

3. Whisk the eggs in the mixing bowl. Roll out the puff pastry.

4. Spread the pressure cooker basket with the butter and transfer the dough to there.

5. Add grated zucchini and chopped onions, and sprinkle the vegetable mixture with the salt and paprika.

6. Chop the dill and add it to the quiche. Sprinkle the dish with the grated cheese and egg mixture, and pour the cream on top.

7. Close the pressure cooker lid, and set the mode to "Steam."

8. Cook the quiche for 40 minutes.

9. When the cooking time ends, check if the dish is cooked and remove it from the pressure cooker. Let the dish cool briefly and serve.

Nutrition: calories 398, fat 28.4, fiber 2, carbs 25.82, protein 12

Almond Pumpkin Cook

Prep time: 10 minutes

Cooking time: 15 minutes

Servings: 5

Ingredients:

- 1 cup almond milk
- 1 cup of water
- 1 pound pumpkin
- 1 teaspoon cinnamon
- ½ teaspoon cardamom
- ½ teaspoon turmeric
- ⅓ cup coconut flakes
- 2 teaspoons Erythritol

Directions:

1. Peel the pumpkin and chop it roughly.

2. Transfer the chopped pumpkin in the pressure cooker and add almond milk and water. Sprinkle the mixture with the cinnamon, cardamom, turmeric, and Erythritol.

3. Add coconut flakes and stir the mixture well.

4. Close the pressure cooker lid, and set the mode to "Sauté." Cook for 15 minutes.

5. When the cooking time ends, blend the mixture until smooth using a hand blender.

6. Ladle the pumpkin in the serving bowls and serve.

Nutrition: calories 163, fat 13.5, fiber 4.5, carbs 13.1, protein 2.3

Tomato Omelet

Prep time: 8 minutes

Cooking time: 9 minutes

Servings: 6

Ingredients:

- 5 eggs

- ½ cup of coconut milk

- 4 tablespoons tomato paste

- 1 teaspoon salt

- 1 tablespoon turmeric

- ½ cup cilantro

- 1 tablespoon butter

- 4 ounces Parmesan cheese

Directions:

1. Whisk the eggs with the coconut milk and tomato paste in the mixing bowl.

2. Add salt and turmeric and stir the mixture. Grate the Parmesan cheese and add it to the egg mixture.

3. Mince the cilantro and add it to the egg mixture. Add the butter in the pressure cooker and pour in the egg mixture.

4. Close the pressure cooker lid, and set the mode to "Steam."

5. Cook for 9 minutes. Open the pressure cooker to let the omelet rest. Transfer it to serving plates and enjoy.

Nutrition: calories 189, fat 14.6, fiber 1.2, carbs 4.9, protein 11.7

Poached Eggs with Paprika

Prep time: 5 minutes

Cooking time: 5 minutes

Servings: 4

Ingredients:

- 4 eggs

- 3 medium tomatoes

- 1 red onion

- 1 teaspoon salt

- 1 tablespoon olive oil

- ½ teaspoon white pepper

- ½ teaspoon paprika

- 1 tablespoon fresh dill

Directions:

1. Spray the ramekins with the olive oil inside. Beat the eggs in a mixing bowl and add an equal amount to each ramekin.

2. Combine the paprika, white pepper, fresh dill, and salt together in a mixing bowl and stir the mixture.

3. Dice the red onion and tomatoes and combine. Add the seasonings and stir the mixture.

4. Sprinkle the eggs with the tomato mixture. Transfer the eggs to the pressure cooker.

5. Close the lid, and set the pressure cooker mode to "Steam". Cook for 5 minutes.

6. Remove the dish from the pressure cooker and rest briefly. Let it rest for a few minutes and dish immediately.

Nutrition: calories 194, fat 13.5, fiber 2, carbs 8.45, protein 10

Poultry Burrito

Prep time: 10 minutes

Cooking time: 45 minutes

Servings: 6

Ingredients:

- 6 large almond flour tortillas (keto tortillas)

- 1 pound chicken

- ½ cup chicken stock

- 1 tablespoon tomato paste

- 1 teaspoon sour cream

- 1 teaspoon ground black pepper

- ½ teaspoon paprika

- 1 teaspoon cilantro

- ½ teaspoon turmeric

- 1 white onion

- 2 sweet bell peppers

- ½ cup cauliflower rice

- 1 cup of water

Directions:

1. Chop the chicken roughly and transfer it to the pressure cooker. Add chicken stock, tomato paste, sour cream, and water.

2. Sprinkle the mixture with the ground black pepper, paprika, cilantro, and turmeric. Peel the onion, and remove the seeds from the bell peppers.

3. Dice onion and peppers and set aside. Sprinkle the pressure cooker mixture with the cauliflower rice and close the lid.

4. Set the pressure cooker mode to "Steam," and cook for 30 minutes.

5. Add the chopped onion and peppers and cook for 15 minutes.

6. When the cooking time ends, shred the chicken and transfer the mixture to the tortillas.

7. Wrap the tortillas and serve the dish immediately.

Nutrition: calories 295, fat 10.8, fiber 5.2, carbs 14.3, protein 35.1

Stuffed Buns with Egg

Prep time: 8 minutes

Cooking time: 10 minutes

Servings: 6

Ingredients:

- 3 large keto bread rolls

- 4 eggs

- 7 ounces cheddar cheese

- 1 teaspoon salt

- ½ teaspoon red chili flakes

- ½ teaspoon sour cream

- 1 tablespoon butter

Directions:

1. Cut the keto bread rolls in half. Hollow out the center of the bread half partially.

2. Combine the salt, pepper flakes, and sour cream together and stir gently. Add the eggs to a mixing bowl and whisk.

3. Add the butter in the pressure cooker. Pour the eggs equally into the keto bread roll halves.

4. Transfer the bread in the pressure cooker. Sprinkle the dish with the spice mixture.

5. Grate the cheddar cheese and sprinkle the bread with the grated cheese. Close the lid, and set the pressure cooker mode to "Steam." Cook for 10 minutes.

6. Let the dish rest before serving it.

Nutrition: calories 259, fat 19.2, fiber 3.6, carbs 2.6, protein 17.5

Coconut Frittata

Prep time: 10 minutes

Cooking time: 10 minutes

Servings: 6

Ingredients:

- 7 eggs
- ½ cup of coconut milk
- 1 teaspoon salt
- ½ teaspoon paprika
- ½ cup parsley
- 8 ounces ham
- 1 teaspoon white pepper
- 1 tablespoon lemon zest
- 1 teaspoon olive oil
- 1 tomato

Directions:

1. Beat the eggs in the mixing bowl.

2. Add coconut milk, salt, paprika, white pepper, and lemon zest. Blend the mixture well using a hand mixer.

3. Chop the tomato and add it to the egg mixture.

4. Chop the ham, and top the egg mixture with the ham. Stir it carefully until smooth. Chop the parsley.

5. Spray the pressure cooker with the olive oil inside.

6. Transfer the egg mixture in the pressure cooker.

7. Sprinkle it with the chopped parsley and close the lid.

8. Cook the frittata for 10 minutes at the mode to "Steam."

9. When the time is cooked, let cooked, let the dish cool little and serve.

Nutrition: calories 193, fat 14, fiber 1.4, carbs 4.2, protein 13.5

Zucchini Frittata

Prep time: 10 minutes

Cooking time: 15 minutes

Servings: 6

Ingredients:

- 10 eggs
- 1 cup of coconut milk
- 1 teaspoon salt
- ½ teaspoon ground black pepper
- 1 sweet bell pepper
- ½ jalapeno pepper
- 3 tomatoes
- 1 zucchini
- 1 tablespoon butter
- 5 ounces asparagus
- ½ cup cilantro

Directions:

1. Beat the eggs in the mixing bowl until combined.

2. Add the coconut milk and butter and combine. Sprinkle the mixture with the salt and, ground black pepper and mix well.

3. Chop the zucchini, tomatoes, asparagus, and cilantro.

4. Remove the seeds from the bell pepper and chop it. Slice the jalapeno pepper.

5. Transfer the egg mixture to the pressure cooker.

6. Top with the vegetables and cilantro.

7. Close the lid, and set the pressure cooker mode to "Steam." Cook for 15 minutes.

8. Remove the frittata from the pressure cooker. Serve immediately.

Nutrition: calories 145, fat 11.4, fiber 1.7, carbs 5.4, protein 7.1

Chives Eggs

Prep time: 10 minutes

Cooking time: 5 minutes

Servings: 1

Ingredients:

- 2 eggs
- ¼ teaspoon chives
- ½ teaspoon chili flakes
- 1 teaspoon sesame oil

Directions:

1. Brush the instant pot bowl with sesame oil.

2. Then crack eggs in the bowl and separate the egg whites and egg yolks.

3. Whisk the egg whites until you get soft peaks.

4. Preheat the instant pot on Saute mode for 3 minutes.

5.   With the help of the spoon make 2 rounds from the egg whites in the instant pot and cook them on Saute mode for 2 minutes.

6.   After this, place the egg yolks in the center of every egg white round.

7.   Sprinkle them with chives and chili flakes.

8.   Close the lid and cook the eggs on Saute mode for 3 minutes more or until the egg yolks are solid.

Nutrition value/serving: calories 166, fat 13.3, fiber 0, carbs 0.7, protein 11.1

Bacon Eggs with Butter

Prep time: 7 minutes

Cooking time: 10 minutes

Servings: 2

Ingredients:

- 2 eggs

- 1 tablespoon chives

- 2 bacon slices, chopped

- ¼ teaspoon almond butter

- ¼ teaspoon salt

- ¼ teaspoon ground black pepper

Directions:

1. Preheat the instant pot on Saute mode for 4 minutes.

2. Then place the chopped bacon inside and cook it for 3 minutes.

3. Stir the bacon and crack the eggs over it.

4. Add almond butter.

5. Sprinkle the eggs with salt and ground black pepper.

6. Close the lid.

7. Cook the eggs for 2 minutes on Saute mode.

8. Then open the lid and sprinkle the eggs with chives. Cook them for 1 minute more.

Nutrition value/serving: calories 179, fat 13.5, fiber 0.3, carbs 1.2, protein 13.1

Avocado Boats with Parmesan

Prep time: 15 minutes

Cooking time: 10 minutes

Servings: 2

Ingredients:

- 1 avocado, halved, pitted

- 2 eggs, beaten

- 1 tablespoon cream

- 1 teaspoon fresh dill

- 1 oz Parmesan, grated

- 1 cup water, for cooking

Directions:

1. Remove ½ part of avocado meat with the help of the scooper. You will get avocado boats.

2. In the mixing bowl combine together eggs, cream, dill, and Parmesan.

3.   Pour the egg mixture in the prepared avocado boats.

4.   Pour water and insert the steamer rack in the instant pot.

5.   Carefully arrange the avocado boats in the instant pot. You can cover the surface of every avocado boat with foil if desired.

6.   Cook the meal for 10 minutes on Steam mode.

Nutrition value/serving: calories 319, fat 27.4, fiber 6.8, carbs 10, protein 10

Breakfast Celery Hash

Prep time: 10 minutes

Cooking time: 20 minutes

Servings: 4

Ingredients:

- 4 eggs, beaten

- 6 oz celery stalk, chopped

- 1 cup bok choy, chopped

- ¼ white onion, diced

- 1 teaspoon ground paprika

- ½ teaspoon salt

- 1 tablespoon butter

- ½ teaspoon dried basil

Directions:

1. Preheat the instant pot on Saute mode for 3 minutes.

2. Then add butter and melt it on the same cooking mode.

3. Add chopped bok choy and celery stalk.

4. Then add onion and mix up the vegetable mixture well.

5. After this, close the lid and sauté the ingredients for 5 minutes.

6. Open the lid and mix up the mixture one more time.

7. In the mixing bowl combine together eggs with salt and ground paprika.

8. Pour the egg mixture over the vegetables and stir gently.

9. Close the lid and cook the hash brown for 10 minutes pr until eggs are firm.

Nutrition value/serving: calories 102, fat 7.4, fiber 1.2, carbs 2.9, protein 6.3

Bacon Tacos

Prep time: 15 minutes

Cooking time: 5 minutes

Servings: 4

Ingredients:

- 10 bacon slices

- ½ cup Cheddar cheese, shredded

- ½ cup white cabbage, shredded

- 1 tablespoon taco seasonings

- 1 teaspoon coconut oil

- 8 oz chicken breast, skinless, boneless

- 1 tomato, chopped

Directions:

1. Rub the chicken breast with Taco seasonings well and place it in the instant pot.

2. Add coconut oil and cook the chicken for 20 minutes on Saute mode. Flip the chicken breast after 10 minutes of cooking.

3. Then remove the cooked chicken from the instant pot and chop it.

4. Line the table with paper foil.

5. Put the bacon crosswise on it to get the shape of the net.

6. Then with the help of the round cutter make 4 rounds (tortillas).

7. Preheat the instant pot on Saute mode well.

8.   Then place the first bacon round. Cook it for 3 minutes from each side.

9.   Repeat the same steps with all bacon rounds.

10.   After this, place the cooked bacon "net" on the plate.

11.   Top every bacon "net" with chopped chicken, cheese, and tomato.

12.   Fold it in the shape of tacos.

Nutrition value/serving: calories 401, fat 27.1, fiber 0.4, carbs 3.5, protein 33.4

Mozzarella Omelet

Prep time: 10 minutes

Cooking time: 8 minutes

Servings: 2

Ingredients:

- 2 eggs, beaten
- ¼ cup heavy cream
- ¼ cup Mozzarella, shredded
- ½ teaspoon salt
- 1 teaspoon ground black pepper
- 1 tablespoon fresh dill, chopped
- 1 teaspoon coconut oil, melted
- 1 cup water, for cooking

Directions:

1. Mix up together eggs with heavy cream, salt, cheese, ground black pepper, and dill.

2.   Then brush every mason jar with coconut oil gently.

3.   Pour the egg mixture in every mason jar.

4.   Pour water in the instant pot and insert the steamer rack.

5.   Arrange the mason jars on the rack and close the lid.

6.   Cook the omelet for 8 minutes on Manual mode (High pressure).

7.   Then make quick pressure release and remove the mason jars from the instant pot.

Nutrition value/serving: calories 151, fat 12.9, fiber 0.5, carbs 2.4, protein 7.3

Mustard Cauliflower Bake

Prep time: 15 minutes

Cooking time: 2 minutes

Servings: 4

Ingredients:

- 1-pound cauliflower, chopped
- ½ teaspoon ground black pepper
- 3 oz Parmesan, grated
- ½ cup cream
- 1 teaspoon dried cilantro
- 1 teaspoon garlic powder
- 1 teaspoon mustard
- 1 cup water, for cooking

Directions:

1. Pour water in the instant pot and insert the steamer rack.

2.   Place the cauliflower in the rack and cook it on Manual mode (High pressure) for 2 minutes. Make a quick pressure release.

3.   After this, place the hot cauliflower in the big bowl.

4.   Add cheese, ground black pepper, cilantro, cream, garlic powder, and mustard.

5.   Mix up the cauliflower well until cheese is melted.

Nutrition value/serving: calories 123, fat 6.6, fiber 3.1, carbs 8.7, protein 9.7

Chicken Toast

Prep time: 15 minutes

Cooking time: 8 minutes

Servings: 2

Ingredients:

- ½ cup cauliflower, shredded

- ½ cup ground chicken

- 1 teaspoon butter

- 1 tablespoon coconut flour, ground

- ½ teaspoon salt

- ¼ cup Cheddar cheese

Directions:

1. Mix up together shredded cauliflower and ground chicken.

2. Add coconut flour and salt.

3. Make balls from the mixture.

4. After this, press them gently to get the shape of toasts.

5. Place butter in the instant pot and melt it on Saute mode.

6. Then arrange the prepared cauliflower toast in the instant pot.

7. Cook the toasts for 4 minutes from each side or until they are light brown.

8. Place the cooked toasts in the plate and top with Cheddar cheese.

Nutrition value/serving: calories 156, fat 9.4, fiber 0.9, carbs 3.2, protein 14.5

Italian Casserole

Prep time: 10 minutes

Cooking time: 50 minutes

Servings: 5

Ingredients:

- 10 ground Italian sausages
- 1 teaspoon Italian seasonings
- 4 eggs, beaten
- ½ teaspoon salt
- 1 teaspoon sesame oil
- ¼ cup Cheddar cheese, shredded
- 1 cup water, for cooking

Directions:

1. Preheat the instant pot on Sauté mode for 5 minutes.

2. Then pour sesame oil inside, add Italian sausages.

3. Cook them for 10 minutes on sauté mode. Stir the sausages every 2 minutes.

4. Meanwhile, mix up together eggs, salt, Italian seasonings, and Cheddar cheese.

5. When the ground sausages are cooked, add them in the egg mixture and stir.

6. Transfer the mixture in the baking pan and flatten it.

7. Then clean the instant pot bowl and pour water inside. Insert the steamer rack.

8. Place the baking pan with casserole in the instant pot.

9. Cook it for 35 minutes on Sauté mode.

Nutrition value/serving: calories 424, fat 32.6, fiber 0, carbs 2.4, protein 25.8

Frittata with Spinach

Prep time: 10 minutes

Cooking time: 10 minutes

Servings: 2

Ingredients:

- 2 eggs, beaten
- 2 tablespoons heavy cream
- 1/3 cup fresh spinach, chopped
- ¼ cup fresh arugula, chopped
- 1 teaspoon coconut oil, melted
- ½ teaspoon ground paprika
- ¼ teaspoon salt
- 1 cup water, for cooking

Directions:

1. In the mixing bowl mix up together eggs, heavy cream, arugula, spinach, salt, and ground paprika

2. Then brush the baking pan with melted coconut oil.

3.   Pour the egg mixture in the baking pan.

4.   Pour water and insert the steamer rack in the instant pot.

5.   Place the baking pan with frittata on the rack and close the lid.

6.   Cook the frittata for 10 minutes on Manual mode (high pressure).

Nutrition value/serving: calories 138, fat 12.3, fiber 0.4, carbs 1.3, protein 6.1

Mozzarella Egg Balls

Prep time: 10 minutes

Cooking time: 14 minutes

Servings: 4

Ingredients:

- 4 eggs, beaten

- ½ cup Mozzarella, shredded

- 1 teaspoon dried basil

- 1 tablespoon heavy cream

- 1 cup water, for cooking

Directions:

1.   Mix up together eggs, dried basil, and heavy cream.

2.   Then pour the liquid in the silicone egg molds.

3.   Top every mold with Mozzarella.

4.   Then pour water in the instant pot and insert the trivet.

5.   Place the silicone egg molds on the trivet.

6.   Cook the egg balls for 7 minutes on Manual mode (High pressure). Then allow the natural pressure release for 7 minutes more.

7.   Cool the egg balls to the room temperature and remove from the silicone molds.

Nutrition value/serving: calories 86, fat 6.4, fiber 0, carbs 0.6, protein 6.6

Breakfast Quiche

Prep time: 10 minutes

Cooking time: 25 minutes

Servings: 8

Ingredients:

- 7 eggs, beaten

- 3 oz Gouda cheese, shredded

- 6 oz Feta cheese, crumbled

- ½ teaspoon white pepper

- 1 tablespoon fresh dill, chopped

- ¼ cup dried tomatoes, chopped

- ¼ cup heavy cream

- 1 cup fresh spinach, chopped

- 1 teaspoon sesame oil

- ½ teaspoon salt

- 1 cup water, for cooking

Directions:

1. Pour water in the instant pot and insert the trivet.

2. After this, in the mixing bowl combine together eggs, Gouda and Feta cheese, white pepper, fresh dill, dried tomatoes, heavy cream, spinach, and salt.

3. Brush the round baking pan with sesame oil from inside and pour egg mixture inside.

4. Insert the baking pan on the trivet and close the lid.

5. Cook the quiche for 25 minutes on manual mode (High pressure). Allow the natural pressure release.

6. Cool the cooked quiche for 5-10 minutes and then cut into the servings.

Nutrition value/serving: calories 170, fat 13.3, fiber 0.2, carbs 2.2, protein 10.8

Breakfast Taco Omelet

Prep time: 10 minutes

Cooking time: 35 minutes

Servings: 2

Ingredients:

- 1 cup ground beef

- 1 teaspoon taco seasonings

- 3 eggs, beaten

- ¼ cup heavy cream

- 1 teaspoon dried basil

- ¼ teaspoon dried oregano

- 1 teaspoon butter

Directions:

1. Preheat the instant pot on sauté mode for 2 minutes.

2. Then place the butter in the hot instant pot and melt it.

3. Add ground beef and taco seasonings. Mix up well.

4. Sauté the meat mixture for 10 minutes. Stir it every 2 minutes.

5. Meanwhile, in the mixing bowl mix up together eggs, cream, dried basil, and dried oregano.

6. Pour the egg mixture over the cooked meat and cook on sauté mode for 25 minutes or until the omelet is firm.

Nutrition value/serving: calories 298, fat 22.2, fiber 0.1, carbs 2.1, protein 21.7

Keto Shakshuka

Prep time: 5 minutes

Cooking time: 20 minutes

Servings: 2

Ingredients:

- 2 eggs

- 1 bell pepper, chopped

- 1 garlic clove, diced

- ½ white onion, diced

- ¼ teaspoon salt

- 1 tablespoon marinara sauce

- 1 teaspoon tomato paste

- ¼ cup of water

- 1 tablespoon coconut oil

- ½ cup kale, chopped

- ½ teaspoon ground cumin

Directions:

1. Preheat the instant pot on sauté mode.

2. Then add coconut oil and melt it.

3. When the oil starts shimmering, add diced onion and garlic. Saute the vegetables for 3 minutes.

4. Then add salt, marinara sauce, tomato paste, water, and kale.

5. Sprinkle the mixture with ground cumin and bell pepper. Mix up well.

6. Saute the vegetables for 5 minutes or until they are soft.

7. After this, crack the eggs over the vegetables and close the lid.

8. Saute the meal for 10 minutes more.

Nutrition value/serving: calories 173, fat 11.7, fiber 2, carbs 11.5, protein 7.4

Cauliflower Bombs

Prep time: 15 minutes

Cooking time: 1 minute

Servings: 4

Ingredients:

- 8 oz cauliflower

- 2 tablespoons cream cheese

- 4 bacon slices, cooked, chopped

- 1 teaspoon fresh parsley, chopped

- ½ teaspoon ground black pepper

- ¼ teaspoon garlic powder

- ½ teaspoon chili flakes

- 1 cup water, for cooking

Directions:

1. Pour water in the instant pot and insert trivet.

2.   Then place cauliflower on the trivet and cook for 1 minute on Manual (high pressure). Then make a quick pressure release.

3.   Remove the cauliflower from the instant pot and chop it into the tiny pieces or just mash with the help of the fork.

4.   Place the prepared cauliflower in the bowl.

5.   Add cream cheese, parsley, ground black pepper, garlic powder, and chili flakes.

6.   Mix up the mixture with the help of the spoon until you get a smooth mixture.

7.   After this, with the help of the scooper, make cauliflower balls.

8.   Coat every ball in the bacon mixture.

9.   Store the bacon balls in the fridge for up to 1 day.

Nutrition value/serving: calories 136, fat 9.8, fiber 1.5, carbs 3.7, protein 8.6

Parsley Muffins

Prep time: 10 minutes

Cooking time: 5 minutes

Servings: 4

Ingredients:

- 4 eggs, beaten
- 1 bell pepper, chopped
- ¼ cup fresh parsley, chopped
- ¼ teaspoon ground paprika
- ¼ teaspoon salt
- ¼ cup cream cheese
- 1 cup water, for cooking

Directions:

1.   In the mixing bowl combine together eggs, bell pepper, parsley, ground paprika, salt, and cream cheese.

2.   When the mixture is homogenous, pour it in the silicone muffin molds.

3.   Pour water in the instant pot and insert trivet.

4.   Place the muffin molds on the trivet and close the lid.

5.   Cook the egg muffins on Manual mode (high pressure) for 5 minutes.

6.   Then make a quick pressure release and remove the muffins from the instant pot.

Nutrition value/serving: calories 125, fat 9.6, fiber 0.6, carbs 3.3, protein 7.1

Egg Sandwich

Prep time: 15 minutes

Cooking time: 15 minutes

Servings: 4

Ingredients:

- 4 bacon slices

- 4 eggs

- 1 cup water, for cooking

Directions:

1. Pour water in the instant pot and insert trivet.

2. Place the eggs on the trivet and cook them for 5 minutes on Manual mode (High pressure).

3. Then make a quick pressure release and transfer the eggs in the ice water.

4. Leave them there for 10 minutes.

5. Meanwhile, clean the instant pot and discard the trivet.

6. Preheat the instant pot on sauté mode for 3 minutes.

7. Then place the bacon slices inside and cook them on sauté mode for 2 minutes from each side.

8. Meanwhile, peel the eggs and cut into halves.

9. Place the cooked bacon on the egg halves and cover with the remaining egg halves to make the sandwiches.

10. Pierce the egg sandwiches with toothpicks for convenience.

Nutrition value/serving: calories 166, fat 12.3, fiber 0, carbs 0.6, protein 12.6

Vanilla Oatmeal

Prep time: 5 minutes

Cooking time: 1.5 hours

Servings: 2

Ingredients:

- 2 tablespoons coconut flakes

- 1 tablespoon flax seeds

- 2 tablespoons hemp seeds

- ½ cup of coconut milk

- 1 tablespoon almond meal

- 1 teaspoon Erythritol

- 1 teaspoon vanilla extract

- ¼ cup of water

Directions:

1. Combine together all ingredients in the instant pot and stir well with the spoon.

2.   Close the lid and cook Keto oatmeal for 1.5 hours on Low pressure (Manual mode).

3.   Stir the cooked meal well before serving.

Nutrition value/serving: calories 239, fat 22, fiber 3.3, carbs 9, protein 5.3

Buttery French Egg en Cocotte

Prep time: 8 minutes

Cooking time: 2 minutes

Servings: 1

Ingredients:

- 1 egg

- 1 teaspoon cream

- ½ teaspoon butter, softened

- ¼ teaspoon chives, chopped

- ¼ teaspoon salt

- 1 teaspoon dried oregano

- 1 cup water, for cooking

Directions:

1. Grease the ramekin with butter.

2. Add cream in the ramekin.

3. Then crack the egg.

4.   After this, top the cracked egg with salt, oregano, ground black pepper, and chives.

5.   Pour water in the instant pot and insert trivet.

6.   Place the ramekin with egg on the trivet and close the lid.

7.   Cook the meal on Manual mode (Low pressure) for 2 minutes.

8.   When the meal is cooked, remove it from the instant pot.

9.   Remove the cooked egg from the ramekin.

Nutrition value/serving: calories 84, fat 6.5, fiber 0.2, carbs 0.8, protein 5.7

Hot Jalapeno Poppers Mix

Prep time: 10 minutes

Cooking time: 11 minutes

Servings: 2

Ingredients:

- 5 oz chicken fillet

- 2 jalapeno peppers, sliced

- ½ teaspoon ranch seasonings

- 2 teaspoons cream cheese

- ½ teaspoon sesame oil

- ¼ cup heavy cream

- 1 oz Parmesan, grated

Directions:

1. Chop the chicken fillet and sprinkle it with ranch seasonings.

2. Then preheat the instant pot on sauté mode for 2 minutes and add sesame oil.

3.   Then add chicken and sauté it for 3 minutes from each side.

4.   After this, place the cooked chicken in the bowl and shred it with the help of the fork.

5.   Return the chicken back in the instant pot and add cream cheese, heavy cream, sliced jalapeno, and Parmesan. Mix up well.

6.   Sauté the meal for 3 minutes more or until the cheese is melted.

Nutrition value/serving: calories 262, fat 16.3, fiber 0.6, carbs 2.1, protein 25.8

Cinnamon Pudding

Prep time: 10 minutes

Cooking time: 15 minutes

Servings: 2

Ingredients:

- 2 eggs, beaten
- 1 tablespoon almond flour
- 1 teaspoon coconut flour
- ½ teaspoon of cocoa powder
- 4 tablespoons coconut milk
- 1 tablespoon butter, melted
- 1 teaspoon Erythritol
- ¼ teaspoon vanilla extract
- ¼ teaspoon ground cinnamon
- 1 cup water, for cooking

Directions:

1. In the mixing bowl mix up together eggs, melted butter, and coconut milk.

2. After this, add almond flour, coconut flour, cocoa powder, Erythritol, vanilla extract, and ground cinnamon.

3. Whisk the batter until it is smooth.

4. Pour water in the instant pot bowl and insert the trivet.

5. Pour pudding batter in the baking pan and insert it on the trivet.

6. Cover the pudding surface with foil. Pierce the foil with the help of the toothpick.

7. Cook the breakfast on Manual (High pressure) for 15 minutes.

8. Then allow the natural pressure release.

9. Remove the cooked pudding from the instant pot.

10. Remove the foil and cut the breakfast into halves.

Nutrition value/serving: calories 212, fat 19.1, fiber 1.8, carbs 6.6, protein 7.3

Parmesan Avocado

Prep time: 10 minutes

Cooking time: 3 minutes

Servings: 2

Ingredients:

- 1 avocado, halved, pitted
- 1 egg, beaten
- 1 teaspoon cream cheese
- 1 oz bacon, crumbled
- 2 oz Parmesan, grated
- 1 cup water, for cooking

Directions:

1. Pour water in the instant pot and insert the steamer rack.

2. Mix up together cream cheese, egg, bacon, and cheese.

3. The fill the avocado holes with egg mixture.

4.   Place the avocado in the instant pot.

5.   Close the lid and cook the meal for 3 minutes on Manual mode (high pressure). Then make a quick pressure release.

Nutrition value/serving: calories 410, fat 34.4, fiber 6.7, carbs 10.1, protein 19.2

Cheddar Casserole

Prep time: 10 minutes

Cooking time: 15 minutes

Servings: 4

Ingredients:

- 1 cup ground chicken

- 1 cup Cheddar cheese, shredded

- 2 tablespoons cream cheese

- 1 teaspoon butter, melted

- ½ teaspoon taco seasonings

- ½ teaspoon salt

- 1 cup leek, chopped

- ¼ cup of water

Directions:

1. Grease the instant pot bowl with butter.

2. In the mixing bowl combine together ground chicken and taco seasonings.

3. Then place the ground chicken in the instant pot and flatten it to make the chicken layer.

4. After this, top the chicken with leek and salt.

5. Then top the leek with cheese.

6. Mix up together cream cheese and water.

7. Pour the liquid over the casserole and close the lid.

8. Cook the casserole on Saute mode for 15 minutes.

Nutrition value/serving: calories 222, fat 14.7, fiber 0.4, carbs 4.1, protein 17.9

Cumin Beef Casserole

Prep time: 10 minutes

Cooking time: 20 minutes

Servings: 2

Ingredients:

- ½ cup ground beef
- 1 teaspoon tomato paste
- ½ white onion, diced
- ½ teaspoon ground cumin
- ½ teaspoon ground thyme
- ¼ teaspoon salt
- 1/3 cup Cheddar cheese, shredded
- 1 chili pepper, chopped
- 1 teaspoon coconut oil, melted
- 1 cup water, for cooking

Directions:

1. In the mixing bowl combine together ground beef, tomato paste, white onion, ground cumin, thyme, salt, and chili pepper.

2. Then brush the baking pan with coconut oil.

3. Place the ground beef mixture in the baking pan. Flatten the surface of the mixture.

4. After this, top the meat mixture with Cheddar cheese.

5. Pour water in the instant pot and insert the trivet.

6. Cover the baking pan with foil and place it on the trivet.

7. Cook the chili casserole for 20 minutes on Manual mode (High pressure). Then make a quick pressure release.

Nutrition value/serving: calories 177, fat 12.8, fiber 0.9, carbs 3.9, protein 11.8

Breakfast Creamy Cacao

Prep time: 5 minutes

Cooking time: 15 minutes

Servings: 2

Ingredients:

- 1 cup heavy cream
- ½ cup of water
- 1 tablespoon cocoa powder
- 1 teaspoon butter
- 1 tablespoon Erythritol

Directions:

1. In the mixing bowl mix up together cocoa powder and heavy cream. When the liquid is smooth, pour it in the instant pot bowl.

2. Add water and sauté the liquid for 5 minutes.

3. After this, add butter and Erythritol. Stir well.

4. Saute the hot cacao for 10 minutes more.

Nutrition value/serving: calories 153, fat 16.3, fiber 0.5, carbs 7.1, protein 1.2

Conclusion

Being an excellent remedy both for immediate pot newbies and experienced immediate pot users this immediate pot recipe book boosts your day-to-day food preparation. It makes you look like a professional and also prepare like a pro. Thanks to the Instantaneous Pot component, this cookbook helps you with preparing simple as well as delicious meals for any type of spending plan. Please everybody with passionate dinners, nutritious morning meals, sweetest treats, and also enjoyable snacks. Despite if you cook for one or prepare larger portions-- there's an option for any kind of feasible food preparation situation. Boost your methods on just how to cook in one of the most reliable method utilizing only your immediate pot, this recipe book, as well as some perseverance to learn quickly. Handy pointers and techniques are subtly included right into every dish to make your family request new dishes over and over again. Vegetarian choices, options for meat-eaters and extremely satisfying ideas to unite the entire family at the very same table. Eating in the house is a shared experience, as well as it can be so good to meet entirely at the end of the day. Master your Instantaneous Pot and also make the most of this brand-new experience beginning today!

Lightning Source UK Ltd.
Milton Keynes UK
UKHW050355110521
383304UK00002BA/174